otters

otters

eagle + man

FOUR PICTURES BY EMILY CARR

NICOLAS DEBON

Cedar House	5
Autumn in France	11
Silhouette	17
Beloved of the Sky	23

To Marie

This book is based on *The Complete Writings of Emily Carr* as well as several books about her life and work, especially *The Life of Emily Carr* by Paula Blanchard, *The Art of Emily Carr* by Doris Shadbolt and *Emily Carr: A Biography* by Maria Tippett. Dialogue and events are mostly based on fact although they have been invented in a few instances.

Groundwood Books / House of Anansi Press
110 Spadina Avenue, Suite 801, Toronto, Ontario M5V 2K4
Distributed in the USA by Publishers Group West
1700 Fourth Street, Berkeley, CA 94710

We acknowledge for their financial support of our publishing program the Canada Council for the Arts, the Government of Canada through the Book Publishing Industry Development Program (BPIDP), the Ontario Arts Council and the Government of Ontario through the Ontario Media Development Corporation's Ontario Book Initiative.

ONTARIO ARTS COUNCIL
CONSEIL DES ARTS DE L'ONTARIO

Library and Archives Canada Cataloging in Publication
Debon, Nicolas
Four Pictures by Emily Carr / by Nicolas Debon.
ISBN-13 978-0-88899-532-2 (bound).
ISBN-10 0-88899-532-6 (bound).
ISBN-13 978-0-88899-814-9 (pbk).
ISBN-10 0-88899-814-7 (pbk).
1. Carr, Emily, 1871-1945–Juvenile literature. 2. Painters–Canada–Biography–Juvenile literature. I. Title.
ND249.C3D42 2003   j759.11   C2003-900369-8

Library of Congress Control Number: 2003100429

Nicolas Debon's illustrations are done in gouache and India ink on Arches cold-pressed watercolor paper.

Printed and bound in China

Page 4: *Emily Carr in her Studio* (c. 1936)
Photo by Harold Mortimer Lamb
British Columbia Archives, D-06009

Page 5: *Ada and Louisa Outside Cedar Canim's House, Ucluelet* (1898-1899)
Watercolor, 17.9 x 26.5 cm
British Columbia Archives, PDP02158

Page 11: *Autumn in France* (1911)
Oil on cardboard, 49 x 65.9 cm
National Gallery of Canada, Ottawa, purchased 1948

Page 17: *Silhouette No. 2* (1930-1931)
Oil on cotton duck, 130.2 x 86.5 cm
Vancouver Art Gallery, Emily Carr Trust, 42.3.7 (Photo: Trevor Mills)

Page 23: *Scorned as Timber, Beloved of the Sky* (1935)
Oil on canvas, 112 x 68.9 cm
Vancouver Art Gallery, Emily Carr Trust, 42.3.15 (Photo: Trevor Mills)

Endpapers: Sketches of Indian Artifacts
Pencil on paper (s.d.)
British Columbia Archives, PDP00831

Illustrations were partly inspired by the following paintings:
p. 14: *Bathsheba Bathing*, by Rembrandt Van Rijn [1654], Musée du Louvre, Paris, France; *The Lacemaker*, by Jan Vermeer [c.1664], Musée du Louvre, Paris, France; p. 15: *Three Graces*, by Harry W. Phelan Gibb [c.1909], Lucy Wertheim Bequest Collection, Towner Art Gallery, Eastbourne, England; *Portrait de Madame Matisse à la raie verte*, by Henri Matisse [1905], Statens Museum for Kunst, Copenhaguen, Denmark; *Three Women*, by Pablo Picasso [1908], the Hermitage Museum, St. Petersburg, Russia; pp. 19-20: *War Canoes (Alert Bay)*, by Emily Carr [1912], private collection; *Skidegate*, by Emily Carr [1912], The Vancouver Art Gallery; *Tanoo, Queen Charlotte Islands*, by Emily Carr [1913], British Columbia Archives; *Indian House Interior with Totems*, by Emily Carr [c.1912-13], The Vancouver Art Gallery; pp. 21-22: *Pic Island*, by Lawren S. Harris [c.1924], The McMichael Canadian Art Collection, Kleinburg, Ontario; *Northern Autumn*, by Lawren S. Harris [1922], London Regional Art and Historical Museums, London, Ontario; *Mount Temple*, by Lawren S. Harris [c.1925], The Montreal Museum of Fine Arts; *North Shore, Lake Superior*, by Lawren S. Harris [1926], The National Gallery of Canada, Ottawa; *Morning Light, Lake Superior*, by Lawren S. Harris [c.1927], MacDonald Stewart Art Centre, Guelph, Ontario; *Lake Superior Island*, by Lawren S. Harris [c.1923], The McMichael Canadian Art Collection, Kleinburg, Ontario; *Northern Lake*, by Lawren S. Harris [c.1923], The McMichael Canadian Art Collection, Kleinburg, Ontario; *The Ice House*, by Lawren S. Harris [c.1923], The McMichael Canadian Art Collection, Kleinburg, Ontario; *Mount Robson*, by Lawren S. Harris [c.1929], The McMichael Canadian Art Collection, Kleinburg, Ontario; p. 24: *Indian Church*, by Emily Carr [1929], The Art Gallery of Ontario, Toronto; *Indian Hut, Queen Charlotte Islands*, by Emily Carr [c.1930], The National Gallery of Canada, Ottawa.

FOUR PICTURES BY EMILY CARR

NICOLAS DEBON

House of Anansi Press   Groundwood Books   Toronto Berkeley

Emily Carr (1871-1945)

The youngest of five sisters, Emily Carr was born in Victoria, British Columbia in 1871. A brother was born several years later. Like many children of their time, Emily and her siblings were raised in a strict, formal home with plenty of religious education and prayer.

As a young child Emily (or "Millie" as she was often called) had a strong independent personality. Surrounded by the rugged beauty of Canada's West Coast, she developed a passion for the wilderness and for animals which was to last all her life. She loved to draw and began to take art lessons when she was eight years old. At nineteen or twenty, she went to study art in San Francisco.

Year after year Emily's paintings became increasingly innovative and daring. Sadly, the more unique her style became, the less understanding she received from her family, friends and the conservative citizens in her hometown of Victoria.

Emily treasured the times she was able to be among the native people of the West Coast. These people and their art seemed to give her insights into the meaning of existence that she had not found in her own society.

In the many pages she wrote toward the end of her life, Emily often refers to a sense of spiritual unity between inanimate things and living beings, between art and nature, between religion and art.

Emily Carr was an extraordinarily gifted artist and she is all the more remarkable for being one of the very few women painters of her time. In the face of many challenges she pursued her own vision, basing her work on her great sense of curiosity and respect for the world surrounding her rather than on what was fashionable among artists of the period.

At the age of twenty-seven Emily made a first
sketching trip to a remote native village on the
coast of Vancouver Island. Although racism and
prejudice toward native people were widespread
at the time, Emily did not share in such views.
On the contrary, she was thrilled to be able to
engage in her life-long fascination with West Coast
aboriginal culture. Expedition after expedition, she
slowly built up an extraordinary collection of paintings depicting the richness of West Coast native
life and art.

CEDAR HOUSE

7

8

After learning the rudiments of painting in Victoria, Emily studied art in both San Francisco and London. But living in such a big, bustling city as London was a difficult and painful experience for her. She became ill and had to rest in a hospital for several months. After a few years back in Canada, however, Emily packed up again and, accompanied by her sister Alice, set off for France.

AUTUMN IN FRANCE

14

Even though she felt that her creative well springs had run dry, two of Emily's paintings were accepted by Paris's renowned Salon d'Automne. Following her illness in Paris, Emily moved to the French countryside where she regained her strength and energy before returning home. Back in Canada she opened a studio where she gave art classes to children and embarked on her sketching expeditions once more. But her new work was too bold for many people and, unable to make a living from her art, she gradually gave up painting.

SILHOUETTE

18

19

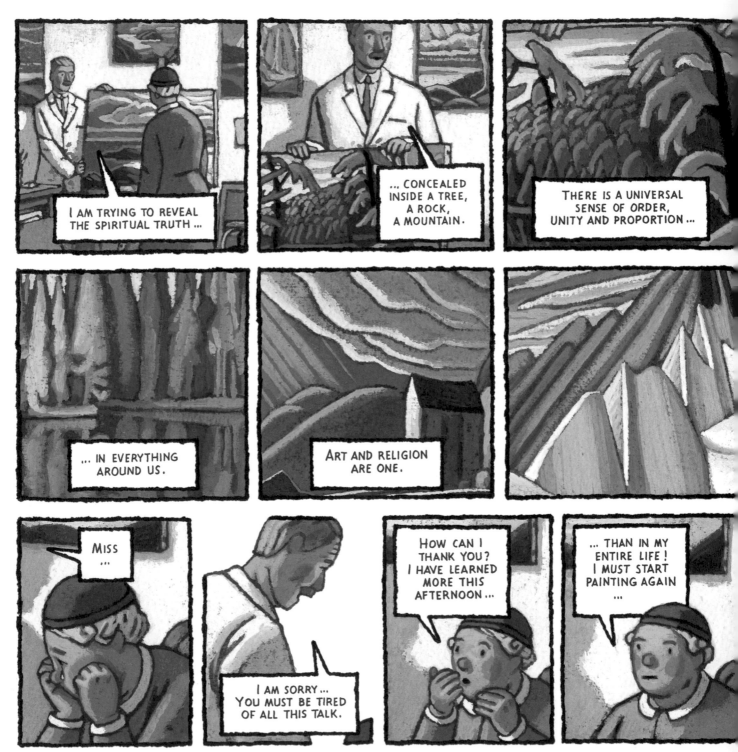

Emily's meeting with the artists who formed the Group of Seven – and in particular with Lawren Harris, with whom she corresponded for many years – was a tremendous revelation to her. In her mid-fifties she now no longer felt alone in her artistic and spiritual quest and, despite failing health, she embarked on a period of extraordinary creativity.

BELOVED OF THE SKY

25

TWO OR THREE TIMES A YEAR, THE "ELEPHANT" WAS HAULED TO A NEW LOCATION WHERE EMILY COULD PAINT AND ENJOY THE WILDERNESS.

... HERE I WAS, FAR FROM THE CIVILIZED WORLD, ALL MY TROUBLES LEFT AT HOME, SURROUNDED ONLY BY MY BELOVED ANIMALS AND THE SOOTHING, ETERNAL BEAUTY OF MOTHER NATURE.

I BATHED IN A NEARBY BROOK AND ATE LITTLE, OFTEN FASTING FOR DAYS ON ORANGE JUICE AND VERY LIGHT FOOD ...

... IT WAS AS IF A NEW, UNKNOWN ENERGY HAD STARTED FLOWING THROUGH MY VEINS.

DAY AFTER DAY, I CARRIED MY DRAWING BOARD AND BRUSHES INTO THE WOODS AND SAT AMONG THE HUGE CEDARS, STARING AND PAINTING ...

THE EVENINGS WERE DEVOTED TO WRITING. THE ONLY SOUND WAS THE GENTLE SWAYING OF THE TREES BEYOND THE WINDOW.

I THOUGHT THAT FINALLY I HAD FOUND HAPPINESS ...

... UNTIL A TERRIBLE THING HAPPENED.

27

THE NEXT MORNING, THE LIGHT WAS SO PURE THAT I DECIDED TO GO OUT AND PAINT.

WANDERING THROUGH THE TANGLES OF DENSE, LUSH UNDERGROWTH, IT WAS AS IF MY DREAM AND REALITY HAD BECOME ONE ...

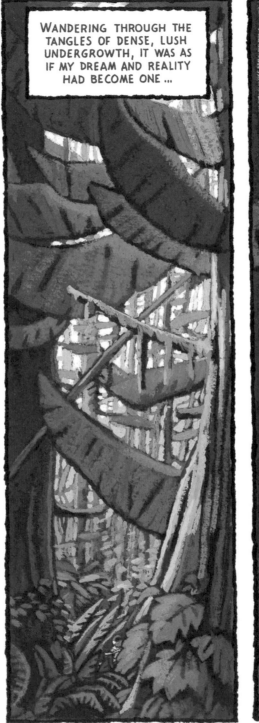

... I FELT THE NEARNESS OF GOD, THE INVISIBLE SPIRIT INHABITING THE LEAVES OF THE TREES, THE ROCKS UNDER MY FEET, THE CLOUDS IN THE SKY ...

otters